DIGITAL MARKETING
THE ULTIMATE
CHEATSHEET

TABLE OF CONTENTS

1. PREFACE

What to Expect from This eBook

Welcome to "Digital Marketing: The Ultimate Cheatsheet," your comprehensive guide to navigating the dynamic world of digital marketing. Whether you're a business owner looking to enhance your online presence, a marketer aiming to upskill, or a student intrigued by the digital realm, this eBook serves as your go-to resource.

Why This eBook?

The digital landscape is ever-evolving, with new platforms, algorithms, and strategies emerging almost daily. Keeping up with these changes can be daunting, but that's where this eBook comes in. We've distilled complex concepts into easily digestible chapters, giving you not just the basics but also advanced tips and tricks to excel in digital marketing.

How to Use This eBook

The book is structured into a collection of multiple in-depth chapters, each focusing on a critical aspect of digital marketing—from SEO and content marketing to paid ads and market research. Each chapter is designed to be both informative and actionable, providing real-world examples and step-by-step guides where applicable.

What's Inside?

- **Introduction:** Get a solid grounding on what digital marketing is and why it's indispensable in today's world.
- **Core Concepts:** Delve into the six pillars of digital marketing—SEO, content marketing, paid ads, email marketing, social media marketing, and affiliate marketing.
- **Practical Insights:** Learn how to effectively target your audience, optimize campaigns, and conduct market research.

A Note to the Reader

Digital marketing is not a one-size-fits-all endeavor. The strategies and insights offered in this eBook should serve as a starting point. We encourage you to experiment, iterate, and find what works best for you or your business.

I hope you find this eBook insightful, informative, and most importantly, actionable. Happy reading!

2.
INTRODUCTION: WHAT IS DIGITAL MARKETING?

The Digital Age

In today's interconnected world, the term "marketing" has taken on a whole new dimension. Gone are the days when marketing solely meant TV commercials, billboards, or newspaper ads. The digital age has provided us with a plethora of platforms to reach our target audience more effectively and efficiently—this is what we commonly refer to as Digital Marketing.

What it Encompasses

Digital Marketing is an umbrella term that encompasses all marketing efforts employing electronic devices or the internet. Businesses and individuals leverage digital platforms such as search engines, social media, email, and other websites to connect with current and prospective customers. Essentially, any form of marketing that exists online falls under the scope of digital marketing.

The Evolution

In the past couple of decades, digital marketing has undergone a radical transformation. Initially, it was all about having an online presence through a website. Fast forward to today, it has evolved into a multi-faceted approach that involves various channels like social media, search engines, email, and mobile apps.

The Objective

While the platforms may have diversified, the ultimate goal remains the same: to attract, engage, and convert customers. Digital marketing allows for more precise targeting, performance tracking, and ROI measurement, making it a preferred choice for businesses and marketers alike.

Benefits Over Traditional Marketing

One of the most significant advantages of digital marketing over traditional forms is its scalability and affordability. Unlike traditional methods that often require a considerable budget, digital marketing campaigns can be tailored to fit any budget size. This makes it accessible for small businesses and startups, leveling the playing field.

The Importance of Strategy

However, having a budget is not enough; a well-thought-out strategy is crucial. Digital marketing is not a one-off effort but a continuous process that requires planning, execution, and optimization. From selecting the right platforms to defining KPIs and metrics, strategic planning can make or break your digital marketing efforts.

The Dynamic Landscape

In an ever-evolving digital landscape, staying updated is crucial. New platforms emerge, algorithms change, and consumer preferences shift. This dynamic nature makes digital marketing challenging but also exciting. It offers endless possibilities for innovation and reaching your audience in novel ways.

Conclusion

As we delve into the various aspects of digital marketing in the upcoming chapters, you'll gain a well-rounded understanding of this field. Whether you're a seasoned marketer or a newcomer, this eBook aims to equip you with the knowledge and tools to navigate the digital marketing world effectively.

3. WHY DIGITAL MARKETING?

The Rise of the Internet

The advent of the internet has revolutionized the way we live, work, and do business. In this digital era, having an online presence is no longer an option but a necessity. This has given rise to digital marketing, a crucial aspect that can make or break a business in today's competitive landscape.

The Scope and Reach

Traditional marketing methods like billboards or print ads have a limited reach and can be expensive. In contrast, digital marketing offers a global platform at a fraction of the cost. Whether you are a local bakery or a multinational corporation, digital marketing allows you to reach your target audience more effectively.

Targeting and Personalization

One of the most compelling features of digital marketing is the ability to target specific demographics with personalized messages. Using data analytics, businesses can now understand consumer behavior like never before. This enables highly targeted campaigns that resonate with the audience, resulting in better conversion rates.

ROI and Analytics

Another significant advantage is the ease of tracking and measuring results. Unlike traditional marketing, where the impact can be challenging to quantify, digital marketing allows businesses to track their ROI meticulously. Be it website traffic, conversion rate, or customer engagement, every aspect can be measured, allowing for data-driven decisions.

The Flexibility and Adaptability

Digital marketing is not a one-size-fits-all solution. It offers incredible flexibility, allowing businesses to adapt their strategies based on real-time results. Whether it's tweaking your email marketing campaign or adjusting your SEO tactics, digital marketing enables quick pivots, ensuring you get the best results.

The Future of Digital Marketing

As we move further into the 21st century, digital marketing continues to evolve at a rapid pace. The rise of emerging technologies like Artificial Intelligence, Machine Learning, and Blockchain promises to transform the digital marketing landscape even further. These technologies offer unprecedented opportunities for automating tasks, gaining deeper insights into consumer behavior, and enhancing personalization.

Sustainability and Ethics

In an era where consumers are increasingly concerned about social and environmental issues, digital marketing also offers a platform for businesses to communicate their sustainability efforts and ethical practices. This not only enhances brand image but also resonates with a socially-conscious audience, thereby creating a loyal customer base.

Community Building

Digital marketing is not just about selling products or services; it's about building a community. Social media platforms provide an excellent avenue for businesses to engage with their audience, answer queries, and offer value-added content. This fosters a sense of community, making customers more likely to stay loyal to your brand.

In this rapidly changing digital landscape, the importance of digital marketing cannot be overstated. It provides an avenue for businesses to reach out to a broader audience, target more effectively, and achieve better ROI. As we explore the different aspects of digital marketing in the subsequent chapters, you'll realize why it's not just an option but a necessity in today's world.

4. Traditional Marketing vs. Digital Marketing

The Historical Context

Long before the internet came into existence, traditional marketing was the go-to strategy for businesses. This included everything from print advertisements in newspapers and magazines to television commercials and outdoor billboards. While effective, these methods were often expensive and had a limited reach.

The Digital Transformation

Enter the digital age, and marketing underwent a transformation as revolutionary as the internet itself. Digital marketing opened new avenues that were not only cost-effective but also reached a global audience. This shift led to debates about the effectiveness of traditional vs. digital marketing methods.

Reach and Accessibility

Traditional marketing methods, although effective in reaching a local audience, fall short when it comes to global reach. In contrast, a single digital marketing campaign can be seen by people across the world, thus exponentially increasing its reach and impact.

Cost Factor

One of the major drawbacks of traditional marketing is the cost. Running a full-page ad in a popular magazine or a prime-time television commercial can cost a fortune. Digital marketing, on the other hand, offers a variety of cost-effective methods like SEO, content marketing, and social media advertising, making it accessible to even small businesses.

Measurability and Analytics

One significant advantage of digital marketing over traditional methods is the ability to track performance in real time. While it's challenging to measure the direct impact of a billboard or a print ad, digital marketing platforms come with built-in analytics. This allows marketers to understand what's working and what needs adjustment, thereby optimizing for better ROI.

Speed and Flexibility

In traditional marketing, once an ad is printed or a commercial is aired, making changes is either impossible or expensive. Digital marketing offers the flexibility to tweak campaigns on the fly. If a particular strategy isn't working as expected, adjustments can be made instantly without incurring additional costs.

Engagement and Interaction

Traditional marketing is generally a one-way street —you send out your message and hope it resonates. Digital marketing allows for two-way interaction. Whether it's through social media comments, email responses, or website chats, businesses can engage directly with their audience, leading to more meaningful connections.

The Hybrid Approach

It's worth mentioning that many businesses find success in a hybrid approach, combining the strengths of both traditional and digital marketing. For example, a TV ad can drive people to a website, or a print ad could feature a QR code that leads to an online campaign.

While digital marketing offers numerous advantages in terms of cost, reach, and measurability, traditional marketing still has its place, especially for certain target demographics and industries. The key is to understand your audience and objectives and choose the marketing mix that best achieves your goals.

5. THE DIGITAL MARKETING ECOSYSTEM

The Holistic View

Digital marketing is not a standalone entity but part of an interconnected ecosystem. This ecosystem includes various components like SEO, content marketing, social media, paid advertising, email marketing, and more. Understanding how these elements interact can provide a holistic view of your marketing efforts.

The Pillars of Digital Marketing

In the digital marketing ecosystem, several pillars work in tandem to create a comprehensive strategy:

- SEO: Ensures your website ranks well in search engines, driving organic traffic.
- Content Marketing: Provides valuable information to your audience, establishing you as an industry expert.
- Social Media: Helps you engage with your

audience and expand your reach.

- Paid Ads: Offers a quick way to drive targeted traffic and sales.
- Email Marketing: Allows for direct communication with your audience, nurturing leads into customers.

The Interconnectedness

One of the most critical aspects of the digital marketing ecosystem is how these pillars are interconnected. For example, a well-optimized website (SEO) can serve as a platform for your content marketing efforts, which can then be promoted through social media channels and supplemented by paid ads. Similarly, the audience you build through social media can be nurtured further through targeted email campaigns.

Analytics and Data-Driven Decisions

The digital marketing ecosystem is not just about executing campaigns but also about measuring their effectiveness. Tools like Google Analytics, HubSpot, and other CRM software provide invaluable insights into campaign performance, user behavior, and ROI. This data-driven approach enables marketers to fine-tune their strategies, ensuring maximum effectiveness.

Adaptability and Change

The digital marketing ecosystem is ever-changing. New platforms emerge consumer preferences shift, and search algorithms update. In such a dynamic environment, adaptability is key. Marketers need to stay updated with the latest trends and be willing to adapt their strategies accordingly.

Automation and Scalability

In today's fast-paced digital world, automation has become a key component of the digital marketing ecosystem. Tools like automated email campaigns, chatbots, and programmatic advertising not only save time but also allow for a more personalized user experience. The scalability of these automated tools means they can be easily adapted to suit businesses of all sizes.

Mobile Marketing

The ubiquity of smartphones has added another layer to the digital marketing ecosystem—mobile marketing. From mobile-optimized websites to apps and SMS campaigns, reaching your audience on their smartphones has never been more crucial. Mobile marketing strategies need to be integrated into the broader digital marketing ecosystem for maximum impact.

Multi-Channel and Omni-Channel Approaches

Digital marketing is not restricted to a single channel. Many businesses utilize a multi-channel approach, involving websites, social media, email, and more. More advanced is the omni-channel approach, which provides a seamless user experience across all channels, both online and offline.

Future Trends

As we look towards the future, emerging technologies like Artificial Intelligence (AI), Virtual Reality (VR), and Augmented Reality (AR) are set to revolutionize the digital marketing ecosystem further. Incorporating these technologies can provide an edge, making your marketing strategies more effective and engaging.

Understanding the digital marketing ecosystem is crucial for any marketer aiming for long-term success. It's not about mastering a single aspect but about integrating various components into a cohesive, effective strategy. As we dive deeper into each of these pillars in the following chapters, you'll gain a comprehensive understanding of how to navigate this complex yet rewarding landscape.

6. BASIC TERMINOLOGIES

If you're new to the world of digital marketing, you may find yourself overwhelmed by the plethora of jargon and acronyms. This chapter aims to demystify some of the most commonly used terms in digital marketing, offering you a foundational understanding to navigate the industry effectively.

SEO: Search Engine Optimization

One of the most frequently used terms, SEO stands for Search Engine Optimization. It's the practice of optimizing your website to rank higher in search engine results, thereby increasing the amount of organic (or free) traffic your website receives.

SEM: Search Engine Marketing

SEM or Search Engine Marketing is often considered a broader term that includes SEO. It involves the promotion of websites by increasing their visibility in search engine results pages primarily through paid advertising.

PPC: Pay-Per-Click

PPC stands for Pay-Per-Click, a model of internet marketing in which advertisers pay a fee each time one of their ads is clicked. Essentially, it's a way of buying visits to your site rather than attempting to earn those visits organically.

CTR: Click-Through Rate

Click-through rate (CTR) is a metric that measures the number of clicks advertisers receive on their ads per number of impressions. It's a key performance indicator in digital marketing, often used to gauge the success of online advertising campaigns.

CMS: Content Management System

A Content Management System (CMS) is software that helps users create, manage, and modify content on a website without the need for specialized technical knowledge. WordPress is a popular example of a CMS.

CRM: Customer Relationship Management

CRM stands for Customer Relationship Management. It's a technology for managing all your company's relationships and interactions with customers and potential customers, aiming to improve business relationships and streamline processes.

KPI: Key Performance Indicator

A Key Performance Indicator (KPI) is a measurable

value that demonstrates how effectively a company is achieving key business objectives. In the realm of digital marketing, KPIs could include metrics like website traffic, conversion rate, and customer acquisition costs.

ROI: Return on Investment

Return on Investment (ROI) is a performance measure used to evaluate the efficiency of an investment. In digital marketing, ROI could be calculated by dividing the net profit from a campaign by the total cost of the campaign.

CTA: Call to Action

A Call to Action (CTA) is a prompt that instructs the audience to take some specified action. It's commonly used in sales and marketing to encourage a purchase, subscription, or other types of conversion.

B2B and B2C: Business-to-Business and Business-to-Consumer

These acronyms distinguish between companies that sell to other businesses (B2B) and those that sell to individual consumers (B2C). Each has unique marketing needs and strategies.

SERP: Search Engine Results Page

The Search Engine Results Page (SERP) is the page displayed by search engines in response to a query. It contains both organic and paid results.

SMM: Social Media Marketing

Social Media Marketing (SMM) refers to the use of social media platforms to promote products or services.

UGC: User-Generated Content

User-generated content (UGC) is any content—text, videos, images, reviews, etc.—created by users rather than brands. UGC can be a powerful form of social proof.

Impressions

In digital marketing, an impression is counted each time an ad is fetched, regardless of whether it is clicked.

Landing Page

A landing page is a standalone web page created specifically for a marketing or advertising campaign. It's where a visitor "lands" after clicking on a link in an email, or ads from Google, Bing, YouTube, Facebook, Instagram, Twitter, or similar places on the web.

Retargeting

Retargeting is a form of online advertising that keeps your brand in front of bounced traffic after they leave your website.

A/B Testing

A/B Testing involves comparing two versions of a webpage to see which one performs better. It is an experiment where two or more variants are shown to users at random, and statistical analysis is used to determine which variation performs better for a given conversion goal.

Conversion Rate

Conversion Rate is the percentage of visitors to your website that complete a desired goal (a conversion) out of the total number of visitors.

Organic Traffic

Organic Traffic refers to the visitors who arrive at your website through unpaid search results, as opposed to paid ads.

Affiliate Marketing

Affiliate Marketing is a performance-based marketing strategy where you reward affiliates for driving traffic or sales to your website through the affiliate's marketing efforts.

Geo-Targeting

Geo-targeting involves delivering different content or advertisements to a website user based on his or her geographic location.

Influencer Marketing

Influencer Marketing focuses on using key leaders, or influencers, to drive your brand's message to a broader market. Rather than marketing directly to a large group, you inspire or hire influencers to get the word out for you.

Bounce Rate

Bounce Rate is the percentage of visitors to a website who navigate away from the site after viewing only one page.

Viral Marketing

Viral Marketing is a marketing strategy that focuses on spreading information and opinions about a product or service from person to person, especially by using unconventional means such as social media.

Native Advertising

Native Advertising refers to ads that are primarily content-led and featured on a platform alongside other, non-paid content. They match the form and function of the platform they appear on but are labeled as "sponsored."

Keywords

Keywords are the words and phrases that internet users type into a search box of a search engine, such as Google, to find what websites match what they are looking for.

Understanding the basic terminologies can significantly ease your journey into digital marketing. While this chapter provides a foundational overview, each term will be explored in greater depth in the subsequent chapters, offering you a more comprehensive understanding of this dynamic field.

7. SEO (SEARCH ENGINE OPTIMIZATION): INTRODUCTION

What is SEO?

Search Engine Optimization, commonly known as SEO, is the practice of enhancing a website or online content so that a search engine will show it as a top result for searches of a specific keyword. In simpler terms, it's about making your website more visible in the organic search results.

The Importance of SEO

In today's digital world, the vast majority of online experiences begin with a search engine. If you want to attract more free Internet traffic, it's imperative to understand and apply the principles of SEO.

How SEO Works

Search engines use algorithms to scan and index

websites. Factors like keywords, backlinks, and user experience are taken into account to rank these websites in search results for specific queries. The better your website performs on these metrics, the higher it ranks, thus attracting more visitors.

On-Page vs. Off-Page SEO

There are two main categories of SEO: On-Page and Off-Page. On-page SEO refers to the elements on your own website that you can optimize, such as headlines, page speed, and internal linking. Off-page SEO focuses on variables that occur off your website, like backlinks from other sites.

The Role of Keywords

Keywords play a critical role in SEO. These are the terms that users type into search engines. By optimizing your website for relevant keywords, you increase the likelihood of ranking higher in search results.

Algorithm Updates

Search engines continually update their algorithms to provide the best possible search results. Staying updated on these changes and adapting your SEO strategy accordingly is essential for long-term success.

Practical Steps and Tools
To practically implement SEO, several tools and techniques can be invaluable:

- Keyword Research: Use tools like Google Keyword Planner or SEMrush to find keywords relevant to your business.
- Competitor Analysis: Tools like Moz and Ahrefs can help you analyze what keywords your competitors are ranking for.
- On-Site Optimization: Make sure to include your target keywords in the title tags, meta descriptions, and content.
- Quality Content: Writing in-depth, quality content not only provides value to the reader but also increases your site's authority and relevance.

Real-Life Example: Local Business SEO

Let's say you own a bakery in Hyderabad. You'd want to rank high for terms like "best bakery in Hyderabad" or "cakes in Hyderabad."

- Keyword Research: You find that the "best bakery in Hyderabad" has a high search volume.
- On-Site Optimization: You include this keyword in your homepage title tag, meta description, and several times throughout your website's content.
- Content Creation: You write a blog post featuring the top 10 pastries you offer, making sure to use your target keyword.
- Backlinks: You get a local food blogger to review your bakery, providing a backlink to your website.

By following these steps, you're more likely to rank higher in search engines for your target keyword, thus attracting more local customers to your bakery.

SEO is a crucial component of digital marketing, affecting the visibility of your website in search engines. It's a complex field that requires ongoing effort and adaptability. In the following chapters, we'll dive deeper into effective SEO strategies that can elevate your digital marketing efforts.

8. SEO STRATEGIES

The Importance of a Solid Strategy

In the previous chapter, we introduced the basics of SEO. However, understanding SEO is just the first step. To truly excel in this field, you need a well-thought-out strategy. A solid SEO strategy not only improves your website's ranking but also enhances the user experience and conversion rates.

Keyword Research and Targeting

- Long-Tail Keywords: These are longer, more specific keywords that are less common but can contribute to a significant amount of your traffic.
- Seasonal Keywords: These are keywords that gain popularity during specific seasons or events, like "Valentine's gifts" or "summer skincare tips."
- Quality Over Quantity: Content Is King

It's not enough to frequently update your website with articles that are stuffed with keywords. The quality of your content is crucial. Make sure each piece is unique, valuable, and well-researched.

On-Page Optimization Techniques

- Meta Descriptions: Write compelling meta descriptions to improve click-through rates.
- Internal Linking: Link your content to other relevant pages on your website to keep the user engaged and to distribute page authority.
- Mobile Optimization: Ensure your website is mobile-friendly, as Google considers this when ranking websites.

Off-Page Optimization Techniques

- Backlinks: Acquiring quality backlinks from authoritative websites is crucial for SEO.
- Social Signals: While not a direct ranking factor, social signals (likes, shares) can enhance visibility and attract more backlinks.
- Guest Posting: Writing articles for other websites can help you gain quality backlinks and reach a broader audience.

Local SEO

For businesses that operate in specific geographic locations, local SEO is crucial. Make sure to claim your Google My Business listing and encourage customer reviews.

Analytics and Adaptation

Using tools like Google Analytics, track the

performance of your SEO strategies. Look at metrics like organic traffic, bounce rate, and conversion rate to assess effectiveness and make data-driven adjustments.

SEO is not a one-time effort but a long-term commitment. It requires constant monitoring, updating, and adaptation. Armed with the right strategies and techniques, you can significantly improve your website's visibility and performance.

9. CONTENT MARKETING

What is Content Marketing?

Content Marketing involves creating and sharing valuable free content to attract and convert prospects into customers and customers into repeat buyers. It's not about pitching your products or services but about providing relevant and useful content to solve your audience's problems.

Why Content Marketing?

In today's digital landscape, consumers are bombarded with advertisements. Content Marketing offers an alternative by providing valuable information that educates the audience, builds trust, and ultimately influences purchasing decisions.

Types of Content Marketing

- Blogs: One of the most common forms of content marketing, blogs provide a platform for you to offer in-depth information.
- Videos: With the rise of platforms

like YouTube, video content has become increasingly popular and engaging.

- Infographics: These are visual representations of information, ideal for summarizing complex data or concepts.

The Content Marketing Funnel

Understanding the content marketing funnel is crucial for creating targeted content. The funnel typically consists of three stages:

- Awareness: Content at this stage aims to attract potential customers. Blogs, social media posts, and informative videos are commonly used.
- Consideration: Here, the goal is to engage the audience by providing more in-depth content like eBooks, webinars, and detailed guides.
- Conversion: At this stage, you aim to convert the engaged audience into customers. Case studies, product demos, and customer testimonials are effective forms of content here.

Content Planning and Calendar

A well-thought-out content calendar can keep your marketing efforts organized. Plan your content topics in advance and align them with holidays, seasons, or industry events for maximum impact.

Metrics and KPIs

Measuring the success of your content marketing efforts is essential. Key Performance Indicators (KPIs) like engagement rate, conversion rate, and

Return on Investment (ROI) provide valuable insights.

Practical Tips for Effective Content Marketing

- Content Curation: Use tools like BuzzSumo or Google Trends to discover trending topics in your industry. This will guide you in creating content that's both relevant and timely.
- Content Promotion: Your content won't generate results if it's not seen. Leverage social media, email newsletters, and partnerships with influencers to broaden your reach.
- Audience Segmentation: Customize your content for different segments of your audience. Use analytics tools to understand the demographics and preferences of your audience for more targeted content.

Real-Life Example: Content Marketing for an Online Course

Suppose you're marketing an online course on "Personal Finance for Beginners." Here's how you could apply content marketing:

- Awareness Stage: Write blog posts on topics like "5 Simple Ways to Start Saving Money" or "Why You Need a Budget."
- Consideration Stage: Offer a free eBook on "Understanding Investments" for people who sign up for your newsletter.
- Conversion Stage: Share success stories

from students who have benefited from your course, complete with testimonials and before-and-after financial metrics.

By crafting content that addresses the needs and questions of your audience at each stage of the funnel, you're more likely to convert them into paying customers.

Content Marketing is a powerful tool for building brand awareness, trust, and engagement. It's a long-term strategy that, when executed well, can significantly improve your digital marketing outcomes.

10. CRAFTING HIGH-QUALITY CONTENT

The Essence of Quality Content

Quality content is the backbone of any successful digital marketing strategy. But what exactly constitutes "high-quality" content? It should be relevant to your target audience, well-researched, and presented in a way that's easy to digest.

The Four Cs of Quality Content

- Clarity: Your content should be easy to understand. Avoid jargon and complex language.
- Conciseness: Be succinct. Deliver your message in as few words as necessary.
- Consistency: Maintain a consistent tone, style, and posting schedule across all platforms.
- Credibility: Use facts, statistics, and expert quotes to establish authority and trustworthiness.

Tips for Crafting Quality Content

- Know Your Audience: Before writing, have a clear understanding of who your audience is and what they want to learn or achieve.
- Use Engaging Headlines: Capture your audience's attention with headlines that are both informative and compelling.
- Break Up Text: Use bullet points, numbered lists, and subheadings to break up large blocks of text, making it easier for readers to digest.
- Incorporate Visuals: Images, videos, and infographics can complement your text, making the content more engaging and easier to understand.
- Call to Action (CTA): Always end your content with a compelling CTA that guides the reader on what to do next.

Real-World Example: Crafting Blog Posts

- Suppose you're writing a blog post on "10 Passive Income Ideas for Beginners."
- Engaging Headline: "Unlock Financial Freedom: 10 Passive Income Ideas You Can Start Today."
- In-Depth Research: Include statistics on the potential earnings for each passive income idea, along with expert opinions.
- Visuals: Use infographics to summarize key points and add images or videos for each income idea to better illustrate the concept.

- CTA: End the post with a CTA like "Ready to start your journey to financial freedom? Download our free guide to passive income now!"

Content Formats and Platforms

Different types of content work best on different platforms. Here are some suggestions:

- LinkedIn: Whitepapers and in-depth articles.
- Instagram: Visual content like photos and short videos.
- YouTube: Long-form videos or vlogs.
- Twitter: Short, impactful statements or news updates.

SEO-Optimized Content

Quality content should also be optimized for search engines. Here are some tips:

- Keyword Placement: Insert your target keywords naturally within the content, including the title and subheadings.
- Meta Descriptions: Write an engaging meta description containing your target keyword.
- Alt Text for Images: Always include alt text for your images, focusing on the content's context.

Real-World Example: Crafting an eBook

Suppose you're creating an eBook on "The Ultimate Guide to Digital Marketing."

- Content Structure: Start with a table of contents, followed by an introduction. Break down each section into chapters and include a conclusion and CTA at the end.
- Visual Elements: Use relevant images, charts, and graphs to support your content.
- SEO Optimization: Although eBooks aren't directly searchable on search engines, using SEO-friendly descriptions and titles can help when you promote it on your website or other platforms.
- CTA: Include a CTA at the end of the eBook, directing readers to related resources or offering a special discount on your services.

Crafting high-quality content is both an art and a science. It requires a deep understanding of your audience's needs, a strategic approach to content creation, and a keen eye for detail. From the headline to the concluding call-to-action, every element should be carefully considered to engage the reader and provide value. By incorporating various content formats, focusing on SEO optimization, and applying practical tips and real-world examples, you can elevate your content marketing strategy to new heights. Remember, in the digital world, content is not just king; it's the entire kingdom.

11. PAID ADS

Introduction to Paid Ads

Paid advertising is an essential component of a comprehensive digital marketing strategy. Unlike organic traffic, which comes from unpaid search results, paid ads allow you to target specific audiences and drive immediate traffic to your website or landing pages.

Types of Paid Ads

- Search Engine Ads: These are the ads that appear at the top of search engine results for specific keywords.
- Social Media Ads: Platforms like Facebook and Instagram allow you to run ads targeting users based on various demographics and interests.
- Display Ads: These are visual ads that appear on websites your target audience visits.

Budgeting and Bidding

One of the first steps in running a successful ad campaign is determining your budget and how much you're willing to bid for clicks, impressions, or conversions. Tools like Google Ads provide various bidding strategies to maximize your ROI.

Measuring Success: Key Metrics

- Click-Through Rate (CTR): This measures how many people clicked on your ad after seeing it.
- Conversion Rate: This is the percentage of completed goals (conversions) to the total number of visitors.
- Cost Per Click (CPC): This indicates how much you pay for each click on your ad.
- Return on Ad Spend (ROAS): This measures the revenue generated for every dollar spent on advertising.

Practical Tips

- A/B Testing: Always run multiple versions of your ads to determine which performs best.
- Ad Extensions: Utilize ad extensions to provide additional information like contact details or links to specific pages on your website.

Types of Ads by Platform

Google Ads

- Search Ads: Appear in Google search results for specific keywords.
- Display Ads: Visual ads that appear on Google's Display Network, which includes over two million websites.
- Video Ads: Run on YouTube and other video platforms within the Google Network.

Meta Ads (Facebook & Instagram)

- Image Ads: Single image ads displayed on the feed.
- Carousel Ads: Multiple images or videos in a single ad for showcasing a range of products.
- Story Ads: Full-screen vertical ads that appear in between user stories.

LinkedIn Ads

- Sponsored Content: Appears directly in the LinkedIn feed.
- InMail Ads: Personalized messages delivered to the user's LinkedIn inbox.
- Dynamic Ads: Customized ads based on LinkedIn profile information.

Twitter Ads

- Promoted Tweets: Regular tweets but paid to reach a wider audience.
- Promoted Trends: Paid hashtags that appear in the trending topics.
- Website Cards: A way to include website previews and calls-to-action within a tweet.

Paid ads offer a direct and effective way to reach your target audience almost instantly. However, it requires a strategic approach, from budgeting to performance measurement. With the right strategies, you can not only increase your site traffic but also improve your overall ROI.

12. OPTIMIZING PAID CAMPAIGNS

The Need for Optimization

Running a paid ad campaign is just the first step. To maximize your return on investment (ROI), continuous optimization is crucial. This involves tweaking various elements of the campaign to improve performance.

Key Areas for Optimization

- Ad Copy: Regularly update the ad text to make it more engaging and relevant.
- Targeting: Refine your audience targeting parameters based on campaign analytics.
- Ad Placement: Experiment with different ad placements to find the most effective spots for your ads.

Testing and Iteration

- A/B Testing: This involves running two variations of an ad to see which one performs better. The variable could be the ad copy, the image, or even the call-to-action.

- Multi-variant Testing: This is an advanced form of A/B testing where multiple variables are tested simultaneously.

Monitoring Metrics

- Quality Score: On platforms like Google Ads, the Quality Score is an estimate of the quality of your ads and landing pages triggered by that keyword in auctions.
- Ad Position: Monitor where your ad appears on the search engine result pages (SERPs) or within a social media feed.

Best Practices

- Seasonal Adjustments: Update your campaigns based on seasons or events that are relevant to your product or service.
- Budget Allocation: Use analytics to determine which campaigns are performing well and allocate more budget to them.

Optimizing your paid campaigns is an ongoing process that requires attention to detail, analytical skills, and a willingness to adapt. By continually monitoring, testing, and tweaking, you can significantly improve your campaign's performance and ROI.

13. EMAIL MARKETING

What is Email Marketing?

Email Marketing is the use of email to promote products or services. But it's not just about sales; it's also an effective tool for building relationships with your audience.

The Importance of Email Marketing

- Direct Communication: Email allows you to communicate directly with your customers, unlike social media platforms where you have to compete with other content for attention.
- High ROI: With a median ROI of 122%, email marketing often outperforms other marketing channels like social media and paid ads.

Types of Email Marketing Campaigns

- Newsletters: Regular updates are sent to your subscribers, often containing a mix of news, promotions, and content.
- Promotional Emails: These are one-off emails aimed at promoting a specific offer or product.

Best Practices

- Segmentation: Divide your email list into smaller segments based on various criteria like purchase history or engagement level. This allows for more personalized messaging.
- Personalization: Use the subscriber's name and other personal information to make the email feel customized.
- Timing and Frequency: The timing of your emails can significantly impact engagement. Experiment to find the best times and frequency for your audience.

Key Metrics to Monitor

- Open Rate: The percentage of recipients who have opened your email.
- Click-Through Rate (CTR): The percentage of email recipients who clicked on one or more links contained in an email.
- Conversion Rate: The percentage of email recipients who completed the desired action after clicking on a link in your email, such as making a purchase.

Practical Tips for Email Marketing

- A/B Testing: Always test multiple versions of your email. You can experiment with different subject lines, content layouts, or calls to action to find what resonates best with your audience.
- Automated Sequences: Utilize automated

email sequences for events like welcoming new subscribers or following up on abandoned cart items.

- Retargeting: Use email campaigns to retarget customers who have interacted with your brand but haven't made a purchase.

Real-World Example: E-commerce Email Campaign

Suppose you run an e-commerce store that sells tech gadgets. Here's how you could use email marketing effectively:

- Welcome Email: When someone subscribes to your newsletter, send a welcome email that offers a 10% discount on their first purchase.
- Product Recommendations: Based on the customer's browsing history, send emails with personalized product recommendations.
- Abandoned Cart Emails: If a customer adds a product to the cart but doesn't complete the purchase, send an email reminder with a special offer to encourage them to finalize the purchase.
- Post-Purchase Follow-Up: After a purchase, send a thank-you email and ask for a product review. This not only builds trust but also provides you with valuable customer feedback.

Email marketing is more than just sending out promotional emails; it's about building and nurturing relationships with your audience. By understanding your audience, segmenting your email lists, and constantly optimizing, you can create highly effective email marketing campaigns that not only boost sales but also enhance customer loyalty.

14. CREATING EFFECTIVE EMAIL CAMPAIGNS

The Blueprint of an Effective Email

An effective email is more than just text; it's a carefully crafted message designed to achieve a specific goal. Here's what goes into making an email effective:

- Subject Line: The first thing your audience sees. It should be compelling and relevant.
- Preheader Text: A short snippet that appears after the subject line, providing more context.
- Visual Elements: Images or videos that complement the text and make the email more engaging.

Content and Structure

- Introduction: Begin with a personalized greeting and a brief introduction to what the email is about.
- Body: This is where you get into the details. Use

bullet points, headings, and short paragraphs for easy readability.

- Call to Action (CTA): Clearly state what you want the reader to do next. It could be clicking a link, making a purchase, or sharing the email.

Practical Examples

- Newsletter: If you're sending a monthly newsletter, include a mix of content such as recent blog posts, upcoming events, and special offers.
- Product Launch: For a new product launch, create an email series building up anticipation before the release, followed by a launch email with a special offer for subscribers.
- Event Promotion: If you're hosting a webinar, send a series of reminder emails with increasing urgency as the event date approaches.

Creating effective email campaigns is both an art and a science. With a clear understanding of your audience's needs and preferences, you can craft emails that not only capture attention but also drive action. From the subject line to the CTA, every element should be meticulously planned and executed to achieve maximum impact.

15. SOCIAL MEDIA MARKETING

The Power of Social Media

Social Media is not just a platform for socializing; it's a potent tool for businesses. With almost 4 billion users worldwide, the potential for reach and engagement is enormous.

Why Social Media Marketing?

- Brand Awareness: Platforms like Facebook and Instagram are excellent for increasing visibility.
- Community Building: Engaging with your audience on social media can help build a loyal community around your brand.
- Customer Service: Many customers turn to social media for quick support and queries, making it an essential customer service channel.

Types of Social Media Content

- Posts and Updates: Regular updates about your brand, products, or industry news.
- Images and Graphics: Visual content like

infographics, product images, or user-generated content.

- Videos: Short video clips or longer formats like webinars and live streams.

Social Media Platforms and Their Strengths

- Facebook: Ideal for community building and brand awareness.
- Instagram: Highly visual; great for lifestyle, fashion, and food brands.
- LinkedIn: Perfect for B2B marketing and professional networking.

Practical Tips

- Content Calendar: Plan your posts in advance to maintain consistency.
- Engagement: Always respond to comments and messages to keep your audience engaged.
- Analytics: Use platform-specific analytics tools to measure the effectiveness of your campaigns.

Advanced Strategies for Social Media Marketing

- User-Generated Content (UGC): Encourage your customers to share their experiences with your brand or products on social media. Feature their posts on your own channels as testimonials.
- Influencer Partnerships: Collaborate with influencers who align with your brand values to reach a broader but still targeted audience.
- Social Media Ads: Use paid social media advertising to supplement your organic efforts.

Most platforms offer highly granular targeting options.

Real-World Example: Social Media for a Tech Startup

Suppose you're running a tech startup that has just launched a new app. Here's how you could leverage social media:

- Launch Campaign: Use Twitter to tease the launch with a countdown hashtag like #7DaysToGo, building anticipation.
- User Testimonials: Share user testimonials on LinkedIn along with a detailed case study to attract B2B customers.
- Instagram Stories: Use this feature to offer a behind-the-scenes look at your startup, perhaps showing the development process or featuring interviews with team members.
- Facebook Community: Create a Facebook Group for users of your app, providing them a platform to share tips, ask questions, and give feedback.

Social Media Marketing offers a versatile platform for reaching a wide and varied audience. By choosing the right platforms and content types, and by engaging effectively with your audience, you can significantly boost your brand's online presence and customer loyalty.

16. SOCIAL MEDIA STRATEGIES

The Importance of a Strategy

A well-thought-out social media strategy is essential for achieving your marketing goals. Without a strategy, your efforts may be scattered, reducing their overall effectiveness.

Elements of a Social Media Strategy

- Objectives: Clearly define what you aim to achieve, such as increasing brand awareness or driving website traffic.
- Audience: Identify your target audience and understand their needs and preferences.
- Content Plan: Outline the types of content you'll produce, including posts, videos, and other media.

Platforms and Tactics

- Choosing Platforms: Not all social media platforms are created equal. Choose the ones that best fit your brand and audience.
- Posting Schedule: Consistency is key. Develop a

posting schedule and stick to it.

- Engagement Strategy: Plan how you will interact with your audience. This could include responding to comments, hosting Q&A sessions, or running polls.

Practical Tips and Real-World Examples

- Content Calendar: Use tools like Hootsuite or Buffer to schedule posts across multiple platforms.
- Analytics: Regularly review metrics like engagement rate, follower growth, and ROI to adjust your strategy.

Example: If you're in the fitness industry, running a "30-day fitness challenge" on Instagram could be a strategic move to engage your audience and promote your brand.

A well-executed social media strategy can be a game-changer for your business. It not only helps you reach a wider audience but also allows you to engage with them in meaningful ways. By setting clear objectives, choosing the right platforms, and continuously optimizing, you can turn social media into a powerful marketing tool.

17. AFFILIATE MARKETING

What is Affiliate Marketing?

Affiliate Marketing is a performance-based marketing strategy where you reward affiliates for driving traffic or sales to your website through their marketing efforts.

Benefits of Affiliate Marketing

- Cost-Effective: You only pay for results, making it a cost-effective marketing channel.
- Extended Reach: Affiliates can help you reach new audiences that you might not have access to otherwise.
- Scalability: As your program grows, so does your marketing reach, without a proportional increase in marketing costs.

Types of Affiliate Programs

- Pay-Per-Click (PPC): Affiliates are paid based on the number of clicks they generate.
- Pay-Per-Sale (PPS): Affiliates earn a percentage of the sale they generate.

- Pay-Per-Lead (PPL): Affiliates are paid for each qualified lead they generate.

Practical Tips and Examples

- Affiliate Networks: Platforms like ShareASale or Commission Junction can help you find reliable affiliates.
- Tracking Software: Use affiliate tracking software to measure performance and manage payments.
- Real-World Example: If you're a SaaS company, offering a 30-day free trial through your affiliates can be an effective strategy to attract new customers.

Advanced Strategies for Affiliate Marketing

- Retargeting Campaigns: Use retargeting ads to capture users who have interacted with your affiliate's content but have not yet converted.
- Custom Affiliate Codes: Provide each affiliate with a custom code to offer their audience a special discount, making it more enticing for them to make a purchase.
- Recurring Affiliates: Create an affiliate program where existing affiliates can recruit new affiliates, earning a small percentage of their sales as well.

Real-World Example: Affiliate Marketing for an Online Course

Suppose you offer an online course on digital

marketing. Here's how you can leverage affiliate marketing:

- Influencer Partnerships: Partner with influencers in the digital marketing space who can authentically endorse your course.
- Content Marketing: Encourage affiliates to create content around your course, such as reviews or tutorial videos, to add value to their audience and drive traffic.
- Performance Bonuses: Offer performance bonuses to top-performing affiliates, motivating them to put in extra effort to promote your course.

Affiliate marketing provides a mutually beneficial relationship between the brand and the affiliate. By carefully selecting your affiliates and monitoring performance, you can generate significant revenue while also expanding your customer base.

18.

UNDERSTANDING YOUR AUDIENCE

Why It Matters

Understanding your audience is the cornerstone of any successful marketing strategy. Knowing who you're talking to helps you tailor your message and medium more effectively.

- Demographics vs. Psychographics
- Demographics: These are factual data points like age, gender, and location.
- Psychographics: These are behavioral aspects like interests, values, and attitudes.

Methods for Audience Research

- Surveys and Questionnaires: Use these tools to directly ask your audience about their preferences and opinions.
- Social Listening: Monitor social media platforms to see what people are saying about your brand or industry.

- Analytics: Use tools like Google Analytics to gather data on visitor behavior on your website.

Practical Tips and Examples

- Customer Personas: Create detailed customer personas to better visualize who your ideal customer is.
- Segmentation: Divide your audience into smaller segments for more targeted marketing campaigns.

Real-World Example: If you're running an online clothing store, you can segment your audience based on style preferences like 'Casual,' 'Business Casual,' or 'Athleisure,' and tailor your marketing campaigns accordingly.

Understanding your audience is not a one-time task but an ongoing process. By continually gathering data and insights, you can refine your marketing strategies to better meet the needs and expectations of your target audience.

19. MARKET RESEARCH

The Importance of Market Research

Market research is the systematic process of gathering, analyzing, and interpreting data about your target market. It provides critical insights that can inform every aspect of your marketing strategy.

Types of Market Research

- Primary Research: This involves gathering new data directly from your audience through surveys, interviews, and observations.
- Secondary Research: This involves analyzing existing data, such as industry reports and competitor analysis.

Market Research Tools

- SurveyMonkey: An online tool for creating and distributing surveys.
- Google Trends: Useful for tracking the popularity of keywords related to your industry.
- SWOT Analysis: A structured approach to evaluate Strengths, Weaknesses, Opportunities,

and Threats.

Practical Tips and Examples

- Focus Groups: Organize focus groups to get qualitative insights into consumer behavior.
- Competitor Benchmarking: Continuously monitor your competitors' marketing activities to identify gaps and opportunities.

Real-World Example: If you're launching a new mobile app, you could use platforms like Reddit or specialized forums to gather user opinions on similar apps and identify what features are most desired.

Effective market research is crucial for understanding your industry landscape, identifying opportunities, and avoiding potential pitfalls. With the right tools and approaches, market research can provide invaluable data that can steer your marketing strategies in the right direction.

20. CONCLUSION

The Holistic Approach to Digital Marketing

Digital marketing is a multifaceted discipline that requires a comprehensive approach. From understanding the basics to mastering advanced strategies, it's a field that continually evolves.

Key Takeaways

- Importance of Strategy: A well-defined strategy is the backbone of effective digital marketing.
- Audience-Centric: Always keep your target audience at the center of all your marketing activities.
- Continuous Learning: The digital marketing landscape is constantly changing, making continuous learning essential.

Next Steps and Call to Action

- Audit Your Current Strategies: Take a close look at your existing marketing activities and identify areas for improvement.
- Implement Best Practices: Use the insights and strategies discussed in this eBook to refine your marketing efforts.

- Stay Updated: Keep an eye on industry trends and updates to stay ahead of the curve.

Final Thoughts

The journey of mastering digital marketing is ongoing. By staying committed, continuously updating your skills, and being adaptable, you can achieve outstanding results and make your mark in the digital world.

Printed in Great Britain
by Amazon

57233222R10040